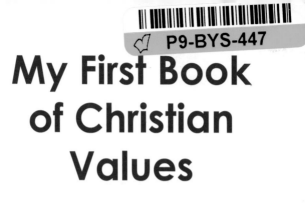

My First Book
of Christian
Values

Carine Mackenzie

CF4•K

Copyright © 2007 Carine Mackenzie
ISBN: 978-1-84550-262-1

Published in 2007, reprinted in 2008, 2009,
2011 and 2015
by
Christian Focus Publications,
Geanies House, Fearn,
Ross-shire, IV20 1TW, U.K.
www.christianfocus.com
email:info@christianfocus.com

The Scripture quotations in this book are based on
the English Standard Version.

Cover design by Daniel van Straaten
All illustrations by Diane Mathes

Printed and bound by
Bell and Bain, Glasgow

MIX
Paper from
responsible sources
FSC® C007785

Introduction

God has given us instructions in his Word about how we should live and what we should say and what we should think.

We are sinful when we are born and we do, say and think things that are wrong every day. But the Lord Jesus Christ, the Son of God came to this earth to save us from our sins.

Through his death we have forgiveness for sins. He lived the perfect life that we find impossible. Yet by his grace our lives can be changed and with his help we can try to live in a way that is pleasing to God. When we fail, the Lord is willing to forgive, if we come to him and ask for forgiveness.

Contents

1. Admitting when you are wrong

Confess your sins to one another and pray for one another.
James 5:16

When we do something wrong, we sometimes try to cover it up or to make excuses and blame someone else. The right thing to do is to admit that we are wrong and to say sorry. It is most important that we admit our sins to God and say sorry to him.

Jesus told a story about a son who left home and behaved badly. When he came to his senses and his need was great, he decided to go back home and tell his father he had sinned. The father welcomed him with open arms. This story shows how God welcomes sinners to himself.

2. Appreciation of others

Outdo one another in showing honour.

Romans 12:10

How often we say "Me first!" We want the first turn, the best seat or the biggest piece of cake. God tells us to think and act differently. You ought to think of:

Jesus   first
Others   next
Yourself   last

If you have Jesus, Others, Yourself in that order that spells out **JOY**.

3. Care about speech

Let no corrupting talk come out of your mouths, but only such as is good for building up, as fits the occasion, that it may give grace to those who hear.
Ephesians 4:29

Careless talk can get you into trouble. Gossip or unkind remarks can hurt another person deeply. It is good to stop and think before we speak about somebody. Ask these questions to yourself.

Is it true? Is it necessary?

God hears every word. Make sure that what you say is true, kind, pure and wholesome. Jesus warned us that we have to give an account of every idle word, in the day of judgement (Matthew 12:36).

Our words indicate the state of our heart. Evil words come from an evil heart. Good words should come from a heart changed by the Lord Jesus Christ.

4. Confidence in God

Trust in the LORD with all your heart, and do not lean on your own understanding. In all your ways acknowledge him, and he will make straight your paths.
Proverbs 3:5, 6

God is in control and does everything well. Even when life is tough and things seem to be going wrong, God understands. When we trust in our own abilities we will make big mistakes.

Peter the disciple boasted that he would never deny the Lord Jesus, but he failed miserably. He was trusting in himself at that point rather than in God.

God has promised guidance and direction when we commit everything to him. Jesus encouraged his followers to believe God and trust in him. "Let not your hearts be troubled. Believe in God; believe also in me" he said (John 14:1).

5. Contentment

There is great gain in godliness with contentment.

1 Timothy 6:6

Be content with what you have.

Hebrews 13:5

Sometimes we can be so unhappy because we wish we were better looking, or cleverer or had more toys or clothes.

God tells us that it is a great blessing to be content with what we have.

Happiness does not depend on things or circumstances. True happiness is from God.

Paul, who had many hardships in his life, could say that he had learned to be content in any situation (Philippians 4:11).

We should pray that we would learn to be content too.

6. Forgiveness

Be kind to one another, tenderhearted, forgiving one another, as God in Christ forgave you.
Ephesians 4:32

If someone does something hurtful or makes an unkind remark about you, how do you react? Do you want to get your own back? Perhaps say or do something unkind too?

God tells us to be forgiving, remembering that we also do and say what is wrong.

We need forgiveness from God through Jesus Christ and so we ought to give forgiveness to others through Jesus Christ.

Ask God to help you to show forgiveness. Jesus himself prayed for those who were nailing him to the cross. "Father forgive them, for they do not know what they are doing" (Luke 23:34).

7. Generosity

Each one must give as he has made up his mind, not reluctantly or under compulsion, for God loves a cheerful giver.

2 Corinthians 9:7

It is good to have a friend who is willing to share with us. If we are mean and selfish, we will be very unhappy.

God tells us to give what we can to others and to him – share our possessions and give our time to those in need, simply and cheerfully.

Jesus tells us to give to others without any fuss - not telling everybody what we have given (Matthew 6:3).

This shows true love. Jesus showed the greatest love by giving us the greatest gift - himself.

8. Gentleness

The fruit of the Spirit is ... gentleness ....
Galatians 5:23

A servant of the Lord must not quarrel but be gentle to all.
2 Timothy 2:24

When God the Holy Spirit works in our heart, he gives gentleness.

This makes us careful and considerate of others who are weak or fragile. We will not treat them roughly.

To be gentle is not a sign of weakness. Jesus, the perfect man, was gentle in dealing with sinners.

He is described as a shepherd who gathers the lambs and gently leads the sheep. To be like Jesus is to be gentle.

9. Goodness

The fruit of the Spirit is ... goodness ....

Galatians 5:22

Let us not grow weary of doing good ... As we have opportunity, let us do good to everyone.

Galatians 6:9, 10

God, our Creator, commands us to obey him and his Word. To do otherwise is sin. We are born as sinners and do, say and think what is sinful.

God, through Jesus Christ, deals with our sinful natures and actions. Only with his help can we do what is good. Jesus tells us to do good to others – feed, clothe, visit – and in doing good to others we are doing it for him.

10. Hard Work

Whatever you do, work heartily, as for the Lord and not for men.
Colossians 3:23

Do you only work well in class when the teacher is watching you? Do you have to be told several times to do a task before you set to it? That is not pleasing to God. He wants us to work diligently and do our best for him.

The little ant is commended in the book of Proverbs for being busy and working hard. We would be wise to be like that (Proverbs 6:6).

The work that needs our attention most of all is prayer and studying God's Word.

11. Helpfulness

Bear one another's burdens, and so fulfil the law of Christ.
Galatians 6:2

Our help is from God. He is a very present help in trouble. He can use people like us to give the needed help.

Jesus told a story about a traveller who was attacked by robbers on the road. The first two men who came by (a priest and a Levite) did not help at all. Then a Samaritan man came along. He helped the injured man, dressed his wounds and took him to an inn to recover – paying for his board and lodgings. Jesus commended this behaviour to us. The Samaritan was a true helpful friend.

12. Honesty

Whatever is true or honest ...
think on these things.
Philippians 4:8

God requires us to be honest and true in
our dealings with others – in our words
and actions. In school it is wrong to cheat
or copy answers in an exam. We should be
honest in the way we spend our money.

When we work for an employer we should
be honest about the way we spend our
time – not using the boss's time for

doing our own business. Other people may not discover a dishonest action, but God always knows – even our dishonest thoughts.

Ask him to help you to make the right choices and to be honest.

13. Honouring your parents

Honour your father and your mother.

Exodus 20:12

Children, obey your parents in the Lord, for this is right.

Ephesians 6:1

One of God's Ten Commandments is to honour your father and your mother. This means showing them respect and obeying them.

The Lord Jesus showed respect to Mary and Joseph and was obedient to them. Even when he was dying he had great concern for his mother, asking his friend John to take care of her.

It displeases God when we are cheeky to our parents or disobey them or complain about what they ask us to do. God tells us to listen to the instruction of our father and to keep the law of our mother (Proverbs 1:8).

14. Humility

God opposes the proud, but gives grace to the humble.
James 4:6

How easy it is to be proud of what we do. We often think too highly of ourselves. We should learn from Jesus Christ who was lowly in heart. He took the place of the servant, washing the disciples' feet.

One day Jesus called over a little child. "Whoever humbles himself like this little child" he said , "will be the greatest in the kingdom of heaven" (Matthew 18:4).

Jesus is the greatest example of humility. As the Son of God, he humbled himself and came to our wicked world as a baby, and died on the cross to save his people from their sins.

15. Joy

The fruit of the Spirit is ... joy ....
Galatians 5:22

Restore to me the joy of your salvation.
Psalm 51:12

True joy or happiness comes from God. Even when times are hard, or we are sick or lonely, we can experience joy in our hearts when we remember that God is in control and he does everything well.

One great reason to have joy is the fact that our sins are forgiven, when we trust in Christ Jesus and what he has done for us.

Heaven will be a place of perfect joy. "You have made known to me the path of life; you will fill me with joy in your presence, with eternal pleasures at your right hand" (Psalm 16:11).

16. Kindness

Love is patient and kind.
1 Corinthians 13:4

One evidence of God's love in our hearts is kindness. Joseph was treated very badly by his brothers but years later he became a very important man in Egypt. Because he was so powerful he could easily have punished his brothers, but instead he was kind to them. "I will look after you and your little ones," he told them. He spoke kindly to them (Genesis 50:21).

Kindness is more than just giving someone a gift. It involves an attitude of love and willingness to forgive, like Joseph. The Lord has forgiven us so much, so we should forgive others.

17. Love

The fruit of the Spirit is love ...
Galatians 5:22

Let us love one another, for love is from God.
1 John 4:7

"Actions speak louder than words" is a very true saying. Showing real Christian love is more than just saying "I love you". It requires giving willing and costly service to another person - putting ourselves out in doing something for them.

Jesus tells us that we even have to love our enemies. If we are able to pray for them and wish them well, then we are showing them the love of Christ.

Our first duty is to love God with all our heart, soul, strength and mind. We love him because he first loved us. Our second duty is to love our neighbour as ourselves.

18. Loyalty

A faithful man will abound with blessings.
Proverbs 28:20

A true friend is loyal and constant. Our first loyalty is to God. He wishes us to be loyal and true to our family and friends.

Ruth showed great loyalty to her widowed mother-in-law, Naomi. "Don't ask me to leave you," she said. "Where you go, I will go; where you stay I will stay. Your people will be my people; and your God, my God" (Ruth 1:16).

A true friend will help in times of trouble and support even when others are critical and nasty.

19. Meekness

Blessed are the meek, for they shall inherit the earth.

Matthew 5:5

When you have a problem do you lash out and make a fuss? Or are you meek, showing restraint and patient self-control? Meekness is not weakness. It requires strength of character and help from God.

Jesus told us to learn from him and to follow him – for he is meek and lowly in heart. He is the best example for us. He has lived the perfect life for us.

20. Obedience

You shall walk after the LORD your God and fear him, and keep his commandments and obey his voice.

Deuteronomy 13:4

God requires us to obey his Word. He has given us the Bible to guide us. King Saul did not obey God's commands, instead he kept some animals to sacrifice to God. But God was not pleased with him. "To obey is better than sacrifice", Saul was told (1 Samuel 15:22).

Jesus told the story of the two men who each built a house. The wise man built his house on the rock. His house was strong enough to stand during the rain and storm. The man who hears God's words and does them is like that wise man.

We should pray for understanding and willingness to obey God's law.

21. Patience

The fruit of the Spirit is ... patience ....
Galatians 5:22

Be still before the LORD and wait patiently for him.
Psalm 37:7

If you are playing a game with your friends it is good to wait for your turn without becoming upset. If Mum or Dad has promised to take you swimming later on, you should not keep pestering them and asking again and again if it is time to go yet.

If we show patience then we will wait quietly. We must also wait patiently for God's answer to prayer. Sometimes he says "No"; sometimes "Yes" and at other times he says, "Just wait for a bit, my time is best."

Job waited patiently for God to deliver him from his hard situation. He lost his family, his property and his health. But he did not complain. He trusted patiently in God.

22. Peace

The fruit of the Spirit is ...
peace ....
Galatians 5:22

The peace of God, which surpasses all understanding, will guard your hearts and your minds in Christ Jesus.
Philippians 4:7

Sometimes life can be rough and difficult – perhaps we get into trouble with the teacher or fall out with our friend. It feels just like being in a storm. We can be afraid, sick, lonely or sad. But if we trust in the Lord Jesus he gives us inner peace in the middle of our stormy life. He gives us the confidence to know that God reigns and that he is able and willing to do what is best for his children.

Joseph had many problems when he was taken to Egypt. He suffered slavery, being falsely accused and sent to prison. But God was with him. God meant it all for good.

23. Purity

So flee youthful passions and pursue righteousness, faith, love, and peace, along with those who call on the Lord from a pure heart.

2 Timothy 2:22

Be careful about what goes into your mind. God tells us to fix our thoughts on what is true, honourable, right, pure, lovely and admirable (Philippians 4:8). If our minds are taken up with impure thoughts, our actions will soon follow.

Joseph was a slave in Egypt in Potiphar's house, but the Lord was with him. Potiphar's wife was a scheming woman who tried to trick Joseph into impure behaviour. Joseph fled from the room to escape. "How can I do this great wickedness and sin against God?" he asked. God was important in his life and uppermost in his thoughts and he was helped to flee from youthful passions.

24. Respect for authority

Let every person be subject to the governing authorities. For there is no authority except from God, and those that exist have been instituted by God.

Romans 13:1

God has placed us in ordered societies which is a great benefit to us. The rules of the land are made for our good and safety, and to help us to live peaceably with other people.

It is our duty to pray for those in authority that they would be given wisdom to rule well.

David showed respect for Saul because he was the king. Saul was an enemy of David, but when David had the chance to retaliate, he showed respect for Saul and did not harm him.

25. Respect for life

God created man in his own image, in the image of God he created him; male and female he created them.

Genesis 1:27

I praise you, for I am fearfully and wonderfully made.

Psalm 139:14

Human life is valuable, a special part of God's creation not just another animal.

We must do all we can to protect life and to respect it.

God has given gifts and talents to doctors and surgeons and others in the medical professions, to care for life and to heal many diseases.

God alone decides the time of our death. "It is appointed to men once to die." Death and life are in God's control.

26. Right choices

Choose this day whom you will serve, but as for me and my house, we will serve the LORD.
Joshua 24:15

We make choices every day. If we make a wrong choice, that can lead to problems. Choosing bad company or taking a foolish risk can lead to danger.

Making right choices day by day will help us to make right choices at the important crossroads in our lives. Ask God to help you in your little decisions and in the big ones.

27. Self-control

The fruit of the Spirit is ... self-control ....

Galatians 5:23

Let every person be quick to hear, slow to speak, slow to anger.

James 1:19

How easy it is to give in to our bad temper or sinful passions and let them control our behaviour and words. To exercise self-control we must be under God's control. Ask him to control your life so that your actions, thoughts and feelings are pleasing to him and not out of control. Sometimes it is right to be angry.

Jesus was angry with those who were abusing God's house by using it for commerce. He overthrew their tables because he was angry. This was not a fit of temper. He was in complete control.

28. **Sympathy**

Have ... sympathy, brotherly love, a tender heart, and a humble mind.
1 Peter 3:8

Weep with those who weep.
Romans 12:15

Many people in our world have great suffering – hunger, sickness, disability, loneliness. We should try to remember these people, pray for them and help where possible.

God tells us to be sympathetic to those in prison who need our help and love. There are some people in prison because of their love for the Lord Jesus. God tells us to remember them as if we are in prison with them.

Perhaps all we can do is listen to a friend who shares a problem with us, or give a word of encouragement.

29. Thankfulness

Give thanks in all circumstances.
1 Thessalonians 5:18

Giving thanks always and for everything to God the Father in the name of our Lord Jesus Christ.
Ephesians 5:20

If someone offers you a gift, how rude it would be to take it without saying thank you. God our loving Father has given us many marvellous gifts – family, home, friends . Remember to thank him. Jesus once healed ten men who had a terrible skin disease. Only one of these men came back to say thank you and Jesus noticed that. The most wonderful gift that God has given us is the Saviour, the Lord Jesus Christ. Thank God for Jesus, the best gift ever.

30. Truthfulness

Whoever speaks the truth gives honest evidence, but a false witness utters deceit.
Proverbs 12:17

God warns us about the dangers of telling lies. The words we speak should be true. We are guided to know what is true by the Bible, God's Word. It is the truth.

Jesus told us that he was "the truth". If we trust in him and follow his Word we will be helped to know the truth and to tell the truth.

31. Wisdom

The fear of the LORD is the beginning of wisdom.
Proverbs 9:10

Wisdom is not just knowing a lot of facts and being clever. The wise person puts God first in his life. Wisdom is learned from God and his Word.

Young Timothy was taught the Bible by his mother and grandmother from his early years. This made him truly wise, leading to his salvation through Jesus Christ.

Memory record

Tick each book once you have learned each
Christian value.

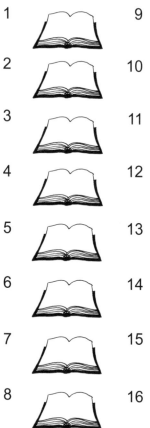

1

2

3

4

5

6

7

8

9

10

11

12

13

14

15

16

Memory record

Tick each book once you have learned each Christian value.

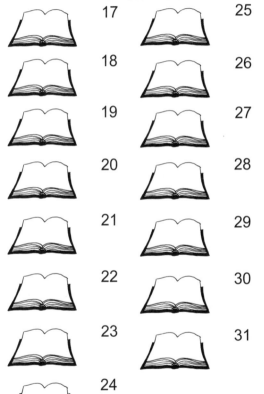

17

18

19

20

21

22

23

24

25

26

27

28

29

30

31

CHRISTIAN FOCUS PUBLICATIONS

Christian Focus | Christian Heritage | CF4K | Mentor

Christian Focus Publications publishes books for adults and children under its four main imprints: Christian Focus, CF4K, Mentor and Christian Heritage. Our books reflect our conviction that God's Word is reliable and Jesus is the way to know him, and live for ever with him.

Our children's publication list includes a Sunday School curriculum that covers pre-school to early teens, and puzzle and activity books. We also publish personal and family devotional titles, biographies and inspirational stories that children will love.

If you are looking for quality Bible teaching for children then we have an excellent range of Bible stories and age-specific theological books.

From pre-school board books to teenage apologetics, we have it covered!

Find us at our web page:
www.christianfocus.com

CF4 •K
Because you're never
too young to know Jesus